Should Christians Always Submit to the Government?

Does Scripture Ever Permit Believers to Resist Tyrannical Leaders?

Dr. Jonathan Mayhew

Edited and introduced by
Stephen A. Flick, PhD

Christian Heritage Press

Should Christians Always Submit to the Government?

Does Scripture Ever Permit Believers to Resist Tyrannical Leaders?

Dr. Jonathan Mayhew

Published by:
Christian Heritage Fellowship, Inc.
1121 N. Charles G. Seivers Blvd, #143
Clinton, TN 37717

Cover Design: Stephen A. Flick

ISBN-13: 9798434852128

Printed in USA

Dedication

To a faithful pastor and loving father,
Rev. Arthur H. Flick

Contents

Image Credits

Arranged Sequentially

Cover: Image Credits style — Monastery of Clonmacnoise, Adobe Images, Copyright.

Samuel Adams, by John Singleton Copley, Wikimedia Commons, Public Domain.

Jonathan Mayhew, by American Episcopal Church 1587-1883 by William Stevens Perry, Wikimedia Commons, Public Domain.

King Charles I, by Anthony van Dyck, Wikimedia Commons, Public Domain.

Henrietta Maria, by Anthony van Dyck, Wikimedia Commons, Public Domain.

William Laud, by Anthony van Dyck, Wikimedia Commons, Public Domain.

King Charles II, by John Michael Wright, Wikimedia Commons, Public Domain.

William III of England, by Godfrey Kneller, Wikimedia Commons, Public Domain.

INTRODUCTION

Blame It on the Pastors

The Role of Clergy in American Independence

For many years, Americans have been lectured by secularists and the irreligious who have insisted the Christian faith exercised no or little influence upon the founding of the United States. But the historical facts argue in support of the formative influence that Christianity exerted upon the rise and progress of America as an independent nation.

∞ Pastors and the Revolution

Buried under an avalanche of Marxist and anti-Christian rhetoric, real historical scholarship has demonstrated the extensive influence Christianity exerted upon America's origin. Pastors, influenced by the Protestant Reformation and prominence it accorded to the Bible (*sola scriptura*) were the leading influence toward American independence. Concerning this fact, historian B. F. Morris succinctly stated, "No class of men contributed more to carry forward the Revolution and to achieve our independence than did the ministers of that grand era of liberty."[1]

Samuel Adams

The Founding Fathers attributed a leading role of influence to their ministers as well. Making no comprehensive effort to compose his list of influential revolutionary voices, President John Adams mingled the names of ministers with well-known patriots such as James Otis, Samuel Adams ("Father of the American Revolution"), John Hancock and others—Hancock himself being both the grandson and son of ministers. Among those ministers identified by John Adams as leading voices of liberty were Drs. Samuel Cooper and Jonathan Mayhew.[2]

Additional scholarly research supports the claims of Morris and Adams. In his book *Seedtime of the Republic*, distinguished Cornell Professor Clinton Rossiter identified six leading voices that were formative in the American move toward independence. They included Thomas Hooker, Roger Williams, John Wise, Jonathan Mayhew, Richard Bland, and Benjamin Franklin. Out of the six men,

---

1 Benjamin Morris, *Christian Life and Character of the Civil Institutions of the United States, Developed in the Official and Historical Annals of the Republic* (Philadelphia: George W. Childs, 1864), 334.

2 John Adams, *The Works of John Adams, Second President of the United States, with a Life of the Author, Notes and Illustrations by His Grandson, Charles Francis Adams*, 10 vols. (Boston: Little, Brown and Company, 1851-1856), 10:284.

most American's recognize the name of Benjamin Franklin and his prominence in early America, but few are aware that the first four men in this list were Christian ministers.[3]

And it is the fourth member of this ministerial quartet—Jonathan Mayhew—who is of particular concern to this present study.

℘ Jonathan Mayhew

Jonathan Mayhew

Jonathan Mayhew was born October 8, 1720, in the town of Chilmark on the island Martha's Vineyard, which is today a popular summer resort located south of Cape Cod, Massachusetts. He was a descendant of the great Puritan migration from England to America which began in 1630. Thomas Mayhew—who was the first to immigrate to Martha's Vineyard from England in 1631—became the governor of the island and was succeeded by three generations of Mayhew's who were Christian missionaries to the local Wampanoag Indians. These included Thomas Mayhew, Jr. (1622–1657), his son John (d. 1689) and John's son, Experience Mayhew (1673–1758), who was Jonathan's father. Among those who joined the Mayhew's in promoting literacy among the natives was Peter Folger, maternal grandfather of Benjamin Franklin. To the credit of the Mayhew's, scholars from their schools were the first Native Americans to graduate

---

3 Clinton Rossiter, *Seedtime of the Republic: The Origin of the American Tradition of Political Liberty* (New York: Harcourt, Brace, 1953), 149-312.

from Harvard.

After graduating from Harvard in 1744, Jonathan Mayhew was called to the pastorate of the Old West Congregational Church in Boston where he labored until his death in 1766. Though raised in the Puritan tradition, he rejected much of his Calvinistic heritage[4] and evangelistic practices of the day, placing him at odds with well-known figures such as Jonathan Edwards and George Whitefield. It may be noted that Mayhew, like others in the New England Calvinistic tradition, stressed the unity of the Godhead.[5]

꧁ Submission to Government

Among several writings for which Mayhew is most often remembered, his political work, *A Discourse Concerning Unlimited Submission and Non-resistance to the Higher Powers*, has garnered most attention. This sermon was delivered on January 30, 1750, in response to the one-hundredth anniversary of the execution of **King Charles I**, which occurred Tuesday, January 30, 1649. The execution

King Charles I

4 *Dictionary of National Biography*, First ed., s.v. "Mayhew, Jonathan."

5 As early as 1755, Mayhew rejected the doctrine of the Trinity. Allen Johnson and Dumas Malone, *Dictionary of American Biography*, s.v. "Mayhew, Jonathan."

of King Charles was the culmination of the English Civil War in which the forces of Parliament were arrayed against the royalist forces of the King. On January 27, 1649, the English High Court of Justice declared Charles guilty of attempting to "uphold in himself an unlimited and tyrannical power to rule according to his will, and to overthrow the rights and liberties of the people."[6]

Defense of Charles' tyrannical policies as king began immediately following his execution. A memoir bearing a Greek title, *Eikon Basilike* ("Royal Portrait"), was purportedly written by Charles and appeared for sale.[7] This piece proved an effective effort in defense of Charles and his policies and for his royalist supporters. Following the English Commonwealth under Oliver Cromwell and the Puritan Parliament, the monarchy and royalist supporters were restored to power with the coronation of **Charles II** in 1660. This act further commended Charles I to the favor of the English people. The same year began his reign, the Anglican Church Convocations of Canterbury and York added the "martyrdom" of King Charles I to it liturgical calendar, being annually ob-

Charles II

6 *The Constitutional Documents of the Puritan Revolution 1625-1666*, ed. Samuel Rawson Gardiner, Third ed. (Oxford: Clarendon Press, 1906), 377

7 Pauline Gregg, *Charles I: KöNig Von Großbritannien* (London: Dent, 1981), 445.

served on the day of his execution—January 30.

During the English Civil War, nearly 300,000 lost their lives—nearly six percent of the English population.[8] This fact was regarded as no small matter by the Puritan Parliamentary forces in England. Jonathan Mayhew looked no more favorably upon the memory and policies of Charles I than the Puritans and would not allow nearly a century of ecclesiastical esteem for Charles to mask the King's tyranny.

℘ Well Before Mayhew

Though Mayhew's discourse was delivered more than a decade prior to the differences that resulted in the American War of Independence, tension between English monarchs and the American colonies had arisen nearly three-quarters of a century earlier. Again, the leading voices of resistance to monarchial tyranny in the seventeenth century were pastors, including **Increase Mather** (1639-1723) and John Wise (1652-1725), the writings of the latter being reprinted and distributed by the Founding Fathers concerning a biblical view of taxation and government by the citizens.[9]

Increase Mather

8 Charles Carlton, *Charles I, the Personal Monarch*, Second ed. (London: Routledge, 1995), 304.

9 David Barton and Tim Barton, *The American Story: The Beginnings*, ed. Second (Aledo, TX: WallBuilder Press, 2021), 92-95.

The influence of Mayhew's *Discourse Concerning Unlimited Submission* exercised considerable influence over the reasoning that led to the American Revolution. Many years following the Revolution, President John Adams reflected upon the influence of Mayhew's discourse when writing to Hezekiah Niles on February 13, 1818. In his letter, Mr. Adams specifically described how Mayhew had affected the American colonies:

> ...Another gentleman, who had great influence in the commencement of the Revolution, was Doctor Jonathan Mayhew... This divine had raised a great reputation both in Europe and America, by the publication of a volume of seven sermons in the reign of King George the Second, 1749, and by many other writings, particularly a sermon in 1750 on the 30th of January, on the subject of passive obedience and non-resistance, in which the saintship and martyrdom of King Charles the First are considered, seasoned with wit and satire superior to any in Swift or Franklin. It was read by everybody; celebrated by friends and abused by enemies. ...To draw the character of Mayhew, would be to transcribe a dozen volumes. This transcendent genius threw all the weight of his great fame into the scale of his country in 1761 and maintained it there with zeal and ardor till his death in 1766.[10]

ꟿ The Lord's Day

Throughout the latter part of the twentieth-century America, the observance of Sunday as the "Christian Sabbath" was disregarded with increasing frequency. Various denominations and Christian associations that once legislated against leisure

10 Letter to Hezekiah Niles on the American Revolution, February 13, 1818. Adams, *Works of John Adams*, 10:287-88.

activities and the commercialization of Sunday, increasingly withdrew their prohibitions until secular interests nearly swallowed the sacred reverence of that day.

But, carefully study the attention that ministers and the church of colonial America, and the student of history will be struck by the reverence given to that day. Like a towering memorial, Sunday worship was a reminder to all America of its Christian national origin. The Muslims adopted the pagan use of Friday as their day of worship, and the Jews retained their Saturday Sabbath, but from the apostolic age forward, Sunday has been a Christian memorial both to the Resurrection of Jesus Christ and the assurance of His Return.

In the following sermon, the careful reader will observe the attention that Pastor Mayhew gives to the subject of the Lord's Day in more than one place throughout this work. Wherever the fires of revival have truly blazed, there has been an accompanying interest in this subject. In harmony with the church of early America concerning this matter, Mayhew lends his full-throated voice.

℘ No King But Jesus Christ

Jonathan Mayhew was among the many American clergy of eighteenth-century America who stressed the divine rights granted mankind against the denied rights of the monarch. That the American clergy had stressed divine sovereignty over the sovereignty of the King is evident, not only from their sermons, but in the corridors of the English Parliament as well. The expression, "No King but King Jesus," finds justification in the following debate in Parliament:

> London, April 26, 1774
>
> *An authentic account of Friday's debate on the second*

> *reading of the bill for regulating the civil government of Massachusetts-Bay.*
>
> Sir Richard Sutton read a copy of a letter, relative to the government of America, from a governor in America, to the board of trade, showing that, at the most quiet times, the dispositions to oppose the laws of this country were strongly engrafted in them, and that all their actions conveyed a spirit and wish for independence. If you ask an American who is his master? he will tell you he has none, nor any governor but Jesus Christ.[11]

℘ THIS EDITION

King Charles I was executed by Parliament on January 30, 1649. In delivering his sermon on January 30, 1750, Rev. Mayhew laid hold of the opportunity to delineate what he believed was the biblical teaching concerning civil government and the violation of those biblical precepts by King Charles during his reign. Rather than elevate Charles to sainthood, Mayhew argued that the Anglican Church should remember him for the tyrant that he was. His protest was against Charles' anti-biblical leadership and the fact that such anti-Christian governance was annually memorialized within Anglicanism on January 30, the day of his execution. Given the strong feelings that existed between Anglicans and Congregationalists, it is no surprise that Congregational Mayhew seized such an opportunity to voice his disapproval of the annual observance of a monarch that should rightly be regarded as a tyrant.

---

11 Hezekiah Niles, *Principles and Acts of the Revolution in America; or, an Attempt to Collect and Preserve Some of the Speeches, Orations, & Proceedings, with Sketches and Remarks Belonging to the Men of the Revolutionary Period in the United States* (Baltimore: W. O. Niles, 1822), 194, 198.

Though the main title of this reprint has been changed to *Should Christians Always Submit to the Government,* Pastor Mayhew's, *A Discourse Concerning Unlimited Submission and Non-resistance to the Higher Powers,* has been retained as the main section division within the body. The text of the discourse remains substantially the same with only minute changes to a handful of archaic terms and expressions. The essence of Mayhew's ideas and arguments remain unchanged from his 1750 publication that helped shape America's understanding of the role of civil government. These pages are once again sent to press with the hope that the liberty they once purchased will not soon be squandered by the darkening threat of tyrannical Marxism or similar forms of statism.

— Stephen A. Flick, PhD
Powell, Tennessee

Author's Preface

The Right to Address Human Governance

The ensuing discourse is the last of three upon the same subject, with some little alterations and additions. It is hoped that but few will think the subject of it an improper one to be discoursed on in the pulpit, under a notion that this is preaching politics, instead of Christ. However, to remove all prejudices of this sort, I beg it may be remembered, *that all Scripture is profitable for doctrine, for reproof, for CORRECTION, for instruction in righteousness* (2 Peter 3:16). Why, then should not those parts of Scripture which relate to civil government be examined and explained from the desk, as well as others? Obedience to the civil magistrate is a Christian duty and, if so, why should not the nature, grounds, and extent of it be considered in a Christian assembly? Besides, if it be said that it is out of character for a Christian minister to meddle with such a subject, this censure will at last fall upon the holy apostles. They write upon it in their epistles to Christian churches. And surely it cannot be deemed either criminal or impertinent, to attempt an explanation of their doctrine.

℘ Standing Guard Against Tyranny

It was the approach of the thirtieth of January that turned my thoughts with solemnity to the subject of the slavish doctrine of passive obedience and non-resistance which is often warmly asserted; and the dissenters from the established church represented, not only as schismatics, (with more of triumph than of truth, and of irascibility than Christianity) but also as persons of seditious, traitorous, and rebellious principles—God be thanked, one may, in any part of the British dominions, speak freely if a decent regard be paid to those in authority, both of government and religion; and even give some broad hints that he is engaged on the side of liberty, the Bible and common sense, in opposition to tyranny, priest-craft and nonsense, without being in danger either of the bastille or the Inquisition—though there will always be some interested politicians, contracted bigots, and hypocritical zealots for a party, to take offence at such freedoms. Their censure is praise; their praise is infamy. A spirit of domination is always to be guarded against, both in church and state, even in times of the greatest security, such as the present is amongst us—at least as to the latter. Those nations who are now groaning under the iron scepter of tyranny were once free. So they might, probably, have remained, by a seasonable caution against despotic measures. Civil tyranny is usually small in its beginning, like *the drop of a bucket* (Isaiah 40:15), till at length, like a mighty torrent or the raging waves of the sea, it bears down all before it and deluges whole countries and empires. Thus, it is as to ecclesiastical tyranny also, the most cruel, intolerable, and impious of any. From small beginnings *it exalts itself above all that is called God and that is worshipped* (2 Thessalonians 2:4). People have no security against being unmercifully priest-ridden, but by keeping all imperious bishops, and other clergymen who love to *lord it over God's heritage,* from getting their foot into the stirrup at all. Let them be once mounted, and their *beasts, the laity*[12] may prance and flounce about to no purpose. And they will, at length, be so jaded and hack'd by these reverend jockies, that they will not even have spirits enough to complain, that their backs are galled; or, like Balaam's ass, to *rebuke the*

---

12 Mr. Leslie

madness of the prophet (2 Peter 2:16).

℘ Degrading Influence of Tyranny

The mystery of iniquity began to work (2 Thessalonians 2:7) even in the days of some of the apostles. But the kingdom of Antichrist was then, in one respect, like the kingdom of heaven, however, different in all others—it was *as a grain of mustard seed* (Matthew 13:31). This grain was sown in Italy, that fruitful field. And though it were *the least of all seeds*, it soon became a mighty tree. It has, long since overspread and darkened the greatest part of Christendom, so that we may apply to it what is said of the tree which Nebuchadnezzar saw in his vision, *The height thereof reacheth unto heaven, and the sight thereof to the end of all the earth—and the beasts of the field have shadow under it.* Tyranny brings ignorance and brutality along with it. It degrades men from their just rank into the class of brutes. It damps their spirits. It suppresses arts. It extinguishes every spark of noble ardor and generosity in the breasts of those who are enslaved by it. It makes naturally strong and great minds, feeble and little; and triumphs over the ruins of virtue and humanity. This is true of tyranny in every shape. There can be nothing great and good where its influence reaches. For which reason, it becomes every friend to truth and humankind, every lover of God and the Christian religion to bear a part in opposing this hateful monster. It was a desire to contribute a mite towards carrying on a war against this common enemy, that produced the following discourse. And if it serves in any measure to keep up a spirit of civil and religious liberty amongst us, my purpose is realized.

There are virtuous and candid men in all Christian sects; all such are to be esteemed. There are also vicious men and bigots in all sects; and all such ought to be despised.

To virtue only and her friends, a friend,
The world beside may murmur or commend.
Know, all the distant din that world can keep,
Rolls o'er my grotto, and but sooths my sleep.

—*Pope*

Jonathan Mayhew

Concerning Unlimited Submission and Non-Resistance to the Higher Powers

Scriptural Interpretation

ROMANS XIII:1—7

1. *Let every soul be subject unto the higher powers. For there is no power but of God: the powers that be, are ordained of God.*

2. *Whosoever therefore resisteth the power, resisteth the ordinance of God: and they that resist, shall receive to themselves damnation.*

3. *For rulers are not a terror to good works, but to the evil. Wilt thou then not be afraid of the power? do that which is good, and thou shalt have praise of the same:*

4. *For he is the minister of God to thee for good. But if thou do that which is evil, be afraid; for he beareth not the sword in vain: for he is the minister of God, a revenger to execute wrath upon him that doth evil.*

5. *Wherefore ye must needs be subject, not only for wrath, but also for conscience's sake.*

6. For this cause pay you tribute also: for they are God's ministers, attending continually upon this very thing.

7. Render therefore to all their dues: tribute to whom tribute is due; custom, to whom custom; fear, to whom fear; honor, to whom honor.

⅋ Scriptural Foundation of Government

It is evident that the affair of civil government may properly fall under a moral and religious consideration, at least so far forth as it relates to the general nature and end of magistracy, and to the grounds and extent of that submission which persons of a private character, ought to yield to those who are vested with authority. This must be allowed by all who acknowledge the divine origin of Christianity. For although there be a sense, and a very plain and important sense, in which Christ's *kingdom is not of this world* (John 18:36) his inspired apostles have, nevertheless, laid down some general principles concerning the office of civil rulers and the duty of subjects, together with the reason and obligation of that duty. And from hence it follows, that it is proper for all who acknowledge the authority of Jesus Christ and the inspiration of his apostles, to endeavor to understand what is, in fact, the doctrine which they have delivered concerning this matter. It is the duty of Christian magistrates to inform themselves what it is which their religion teaches concerning the nature and design of their office. And it is equally the duty of all Christian people to inform themselves what it is which their religion teaches concerning that subjection which they owe to the *higher powers*. It is for these reasons that I have attempted to examine into the Scripture account of this matter, in order to lay it before you with the same freedom which I constantly use with relation to other doctrines and precepts of Christianity, not doubting but you will judge upon everything offered to your consideration, with the same spirit of freedom and liberty with which it is spoken.

℘ Subjection to Civil Magistrates

The passage read is the fullest and most expressive of any in the New Testament relating to rulers and subjects. And therefore, I thought it proper to ground upon it, what I had to propose to you with reference to the authority of the civil magistrate, and the subjection which is due to him. But before I enter upon an explanation of the several parts of this passage, it will be proper to observe one thing which may serve as a key to the whole of it.

It is to be observed, then, that there were some persons amongst the Christians of the apostolic age, and particularly those at Rome to whom St. Paul is here writing, who seditiously disclaimed all subjection to civil authority; refusing to pay taxes and the duties laid upon their traffic and merchandize; and who scrupled not to speak of their rulers, without any due regard to their office and character. Some of these turbulent Christians were converts from Judaism, and others from paganism. The Jews in general had, long before this time, taken up a strange conceit, that being the peculiar and elect people of God, they were therefore, exempted from the jurisdiction of any heathen princes or governors. Upon this ground it was, that some of them, during the public ministry of our blessed Savior, came to him with that question, *Is it lawful to give tribute unto Cesar or not?* (Matthew 12:17) And this notion many of them retained after they were proselyted to the Christian faith. As to the gentile converts, some of them grossly mistook the nature of that liberty which the gospel promised, and thought that by virtue of their subjection to Christ, the only King and Head of his church, they were wholly freed from subjection to any other prince as though Christ's kingdom had been of this world in such a sense as to interfere with the civil powers of the earth, and to deliver their subjects from that allegiance and duty, which they before owed to them. Of these visionary Christians in general, who disowned subjection to the civil powers in being where they respectively lived, there is mention made in several places in the New Testament. The Apostle Peter in particular characterizes them in this manner—*them that—despise government—presumptuous are they, self-willed—they are not afraid to speak evil of dignities* (2 Peter 2:10).

Now it is with reference to these doting Christians, that the apostle speaks in the passage before us. And I shall now give you the sense of it in a paraphrase upon each verse in its order, desiring you to keep in mind the character of the persons for whom it is designed that so, as I go along, you may see how just and natural this address is and how well suited to the circumstances of those against whom it is levelled.

℘ Civil Authority Ordained of God

The apostle begins thus, *Let every soul*[13] *be subject unto the higher powers;*[14] *for there is no power*[15] *but of God: the pow-*

---

13 *Every soul*—This is a Hebraism, which signifies every man; so that the apostle does not exempt the clergy, such as were endowed with the gift of prophesy, or any other miraculous powers which subsisted in the church at that day. And by his using the Hebrew idiom, it seems that he had the Jewish converts principally in his eye.

14 *The higher powers*—More literally the over-ruling powers, which term extends to all civil rulers in common.

15 By *power*, the apostle intends not lawless strength and brutal force, without regulation or proper direction; but just authority, for so the word here used properly signifies. There may be power where there is no authority. No man has any

ers that be[16] *are ordained of God.*[17] As if to say, "Whereas some professed Christians vainly imagine that they are wholly excused from all manner of duty and subjection to civil authority, refusing to honor their rulers and to pay taxes, which opinion is not only unreasonable in itself, but also tends to fix a lasting reproach upon the Christian name and profession, I now, as an apostle and ambassador of Christ, exhort every one of you, be he who he will, to pay all dutiful submission to those who are vested with any civil office. For there is, properly speaking, no authority but what is derived from God, as it is only by his permission and providence that any possess it. Yea, I may add, that all civil magistrates, as such, although they may be heathens, are appointed and ordained of God. For it is certainly God's will that so useful an institution as that of magistracy, should take place in the world for the good of civil society."

The apostle proceeds, *Whosoever, therefore, resisteth the*

---

authority to do what is wrong and injurious, though he may have power to do it.

16 *The powers that be*—those persons who are in fact vested with authority; those who are in possession. And who those are, the apostle leaves Christians to determine for themselves; but whoever they are, they are to be obeyed.

17 *Ordained of God*—As it is not without God's providence and permission, that any are clothed with authority; and as it is agreeable to the positive will and purpose of God, that there should be some persons vested with authority for the good of society, not that any rulers have their commission immediately from God the supreme Lord of the universe. If any assert that kings, or any other rulers, are ordained of God in the latter sense, it is incumbent upon them to show the commission which they speak of, under the broad seal of heaven. And when they do this, they will, no doubt, be believed.

power, resisteth the ordinance of God; and they that resist shall receive to themselves damnation. To interpret further: "Think not, therefore, that ye are guiltless of any crime or sin against God, when ye factiously disobey and resist the civil authority. For magistracy and government being, as I have said, the ordinance and appointment of God, it follows, that to resist magistrates in the execution of their offices is really to resist the will and ordinance of God himself. And they who thus resist, will accordingly be punished by God for this sin in common with others."

℘ Opposition to Magistrates is Opposition to God

The apostle goes on—*For rulers are not a terror to good works, but to the evil.*[18] *Wilt thou then, not be afraid of the power? Do that which is good, and thou shalt have praise of the same. For he is the minister of God to thee for good.*[19] I take this to mean, "That you may see the truth and justness of what I assert, (viz. that magistracy is the ordinance of God, and that you sin against him in opposing it,) consider that even pagan rulers are not, by the nature and design of their office, enemies and a terror to the good and virtuous actions of men,

---

18 *For rulers are not a terror to good works, but to the evil.* It cannot be supposed that the apostle designs here, or in any of the succeeding verses, to give the true character of Nero, or any other civil powers then in being, as if they were in fact such persons as he describes, a terror to evil works only, and not to the good. For such a character did not belong to them; and the apostle was no sycophant, or parasite of power, whatever some of his pretended successors have been. He only tells what rulers would be, provided they acted up to their character and office.

19 Verse three and part of fourth.

but only to the injurious and mischievous to society. Will ye not, then, reverence and honor magistracy when ye see the good end and intention of it? How can ye be so unreasonable? Only mind to do your duty as members of society; and this will gain you the applause and favor of all good rulers. For while you do thus, they are, by their office, as ministers of God, obliged to encourage and protect you; it is for this very purpose that they are clothed with power."

℘ Magistrates to Punish Evil

The apostle adds—*But if thou do that which is evil, be afraid, for he beareth not the sword in vain. For he is the minister of God, a revenger, to execute wrath upon him that doeth evil*—verse four, latter part.[20]

---

20 It is manifest that when the apostle speaks of it as the office of civil rulers, to encourage what is good, and to punish what is evil, he speaks only of civil good and evil. They are to consult the good of society as such; not to dictate in religious concerns; not to make laws for the government of men's consciences; and to inflict civil penalties for religious crimes. It is sufficient to overthrow the doctrine of the authority of the civil magistrate in affairs of a spiritual nature, (so far as it is built upon anything which is here said by St. Paul, or upon anything else in the New Testament) only to observe that all the magistrates then in the world were heathen, implacable enemies to Christianity, so that to give them authority in religious matters, would have been, in effect, to give them authority to extirpate the Christian religion, and to establish the idolatries and superstitions of paganism. And can anyone reasonably suppose that the apostle had any intention to extend the authority of rulers, beyond concerns merely civil and political, to the overthrowing of that religion which he himself was so zealous in propagating! But it is natural for those whose religion can-

That is, "But upon the other hand, if ye refuse to do your duty as members of society; if ye refuse to bear your part in the support of government; if ye are disorderly and do things which merit civil chastisement then, indeed, ye have reason to be afraid. For it is not in vain that rulers are vested with the power of inflicting punishment. They are, by their office, not only the ministers of God for good to those that do well; but also, his ministers to revenge, to discountenance and punish those that are unruly, and injurious to their neighbors."

The apostle proceeds—*Wherefore ye must needs be subject not only for wrath, but also for conscience's sake* (v. 5). To interpret: "Since, therefore, magistracy is the ordinance of God; and since rulers are, by their office, benefactors to society by discouraging what is bad, and encouraging what is good and so preserving peace and order amongst men, it is evident that ye ought to pay a willing subjection to them; not to obey merely for fear of exposing yourselves to their wrath and displeasure, but also in point of reason, duty and conscience. Ye are under an indispensable obligation as Christians, to honor their office, and to submit to them in the execution of it."

℘ Magistrates Instituted for Good of Society

The apostle goes on—*For, for this cause pay you tribute also: for they are God's ministers, attending continually upon this very thing* (v. 6). Interpreting once again, "And here is a plain reason also why ye should pay tribute to them; for they are God's ministers; exalted above the common level of mankind, not that they may indulge themselves in softness and luxury and be entitled to the servile homage of their fellow men; but that they may execute an office no less laborious

---

not be supported upon the footing of reason and argument, to have recourse to power and force, which will serve a bad cause as well as a good one; and indeed, much better.

than honorable; and attend continually upon the public welfare. This being their business and duty, it is but reasonable that they should be requited for their care and diligence in performing it; and enabled, by taxes levied upon the subject, effectually to prosecute the great end of their institution, the good of society."

The apostle sums all up in the following words—*Render therefore to all their dues: tribute,*[21] *to whom tribute is due; custom,*[22] *to whom custom; fear, to whom fear; honor, to whom honor* (v. 7). Which means, "Let it not, therefore, be said of any of you hereafter, that you contemn government to the reproach of yourselves, and of the Christian religion. Neither your being Jews by nation, nor your becoming the subjects of Christ's kingdom, gives you any dispensation for making disturbances in the government under which you live. Approve yourselves, therefore, as peaceable and dutiful subjects. Be ready to pay to your rulers all that they may, in respect of their office, justly demand of you. Render tribute and custom to those of your governors to whom tribute and custom belong. And cheerfully honor and reverence all who are vested with civil authority, according to their deserts."

The apostle's doctrine in the passage thus explained, concerning the office of civil rulers, and the duty of subjects, may be

---

21 [See Mayhew's discussion of this term in the following footnote. — Flick]

22 Grotius observes that the Greek words here used, answer to the *tributum* and *vectigal* of the Romans; the former was the money paid for the soil and poll; the latter, the duties laid upon some sorts of merchandize. And what the apostle here says, deserves to be seriously considered by all Christians concerned in that common practice of carrying on an illicit trade, and running of goods.

summed up in the following observations.[23] That is to say, that the end of magistracy is the good of civil society, as such:

℘ Summary Concerning Magistrates

That civil rulers, as such, are the ordinance and ministers of God, it being by his permission and providence that any bear rule, and agreeable to his will; that there should be some persons vested with authority in society, for the well-being of it. That which is here said concerning civil rulers, extends to all of them in common. It relates indifferently to monarchical, republican and aristocratical government, and to all other forms which truly answer the sole end of government, the happiness of society; and to all the different degrees of authority in any particular state—to inferior officers no less than to the supreme;

That disobedience to civil rulers in the due exercise of their authority is not merely a political sin, but a heinous offence against God and religion;

That the true ground and reason[24] of our obligation to be

---

23 The several observations here only mentioned, were handled at large in two preceding discourses upon this subject.

24 Some suppose the apostle, in this passage, enforces the duty of submission with two arguments quite distinct from each other; one taken from this consideration, that rulers are the ordinance and the ministers of God, (vs. 1, 2, and 4) and the other, from the benefits that accrue to society from civil government, (vs. 3, 4, and 6). And indeed, these may be distinct motives and arguments for submission, as they may be separately viewed and contemplated. But when we consider that rulers are not the ordinance and the ministers of God, but only so far forth as they perform God's will by acting up

subject to the *higher powers,* is the usefulness of magistracy (when properly exercised) to human society, and its subserviency to the general welfare;

That obedience to civil rulers is here equally required under all forms of government, which answer the sole end of all government, the good of society, and to every degree of authority in any state, whether supreme or subordinate;

And from this it follows, that if unlimited obedience and non-resistance, be here required as a duty under any one form of government, it is also required as a duty under all other forms, and as a duty to subordinate rulers as well as to the supreme.

And last, that those civil rulers to whom the apostle enjoins subjection, are the persons in *possession, the powers that be,* those who are *actually* vested with authority.[25]

---

to their office and character, and so by being benefactors to society, this makes these arguments coincide and run up into one at last: At least so far, that the former of them cannot hold good for submission, where the latter fails. Put the supposition, that any man bearing the title of a magistrate, should exercise his power in such a manner as to have no claim to obedience by virtue of that argument which is founded upon the usefulness of magistracy; and you equally take off the force of the other argument also, which is founded upon his being the ordinance and the minister of God. For he is no longer God's ordinance and minister, than he acts up to his office and character, by exercising his power for the good of society—This is, in brief, the reason why it is said above, in the singular number, that the true ground and reason, &c. The use and propriety of this remark may possibly be more apparent in the progress of the argument concerning resistance.

25 This must be understood with this proviso, that they do

The Extent of Subjection to Magistrates

There is one very important and interesting point which remains to be inquired into—namely, the extent of that subjection to the higher powers, which is here enjoined as a duty upon all Christians. Some have thought it warrantable and glorious to disobey the civil powers in certain circumstances; and, in cases of very great and general oppression, when humble remonstrances fail of having any effect, and when the public welfare cannot be otherwise provided for and secured, to rise unanimously even against the sovereign himself, in order to redress their grievances;

There is one very important and interesting point which re-mains to be inquired into—namely, the extent of that subjection to the higher powers, which is here enjoined as a duty upon all Christians.

---

not grossly abuse their power and trust but exercise it for the good of those that are governed. Who these persons were, whether Nero, etc. or not, the apostle does not say; but leaves it to be determined by those to whom he writes. God does not interpose, in a miraculous way, to point out the persons who shall bear rule, and to whom subjection is due. And as to the unalienable, indefeasible right of primogeniture, the Scriptures are entirely silent: or rather plainly contradict it: Saul being the first king among the Israelites; and appointed to the royal dignity, during his own father's lifetime: and he was succeeded, or rather superseded, by David, the last born among many brethren—Now if God has not invariably determined this matter, it. must, of course, be determined by men. And if it be determined by men, it must be determined either in the way of force, or of compact. And which of these is the most equitable, can be no question.

to vindicate their natural and legal rights, to break the yoke of tyranny and free themselves and posterity from inglorious servitude and ruin. It is upon this principle that many royal oppressors have been driven from their thrones into banishment, and many slain by the hands of their subjects. It was upon this principle that Tarquin was expelled from Rome, and Julius Cesar, the conqueror of the world, and the tyrant of his country, cut off in the senate house. It was upon this principle that King Charles I was beheaded before his own banqueting house. It was upon this principle that King James II was made to flee from that country which he aimed at enslaving. And upon this principle was that revolution brought about which has been so fruitful of happy consequences to Great Britain.

∞ The Question of Resisting a Tyrannical Magistrate

But, in opposition to this principle, it has often been asserted that the Scripture in general (and the passage under consideration in particular) makes all resistance to princes a crime, in any case whatever—If they turn tyrants and become the common oppressors of those whose welfare they ought to regard with a paternal affection, we must not pretend to right ourselves, unless it be by prayers and tears and humble entreaties. And if these methods fail of procuring redress, we must not have recourse to any other, but all suffer ourselves to be robbed and butchered at the pleasure of the Lord's anointed, lest we should incur the sin of rebellion and the punishment of damnation. For he has God's authority and commission to bear him out in the worst of crimes, so far that he may not be withstood or controlled. Now whether we are obliged to yield such an absolute submission to our prince; or whether disobedience and resistance may not be justifiable in some cases, notwithstanding anything in the passage before us, is an inquiry in which we are all concerned; and this is the inquiry which is the main design of the present discourse.

Now there does not seem to be any necessity of supposing that an absolute, unlimited obedience, whether active or passive, is here enjoined, merely for this reason, that the precept is delivered in absolute terms without any exception or limitation expressly mentioned. We are enjoined, (v. 1) to be *subject to the higher powers,* and (v. 5) to be *subject for conscience's sake.* And because these expressions are absolute and unlimited, (or more properly, general) some have inferred, that the subjection required in them, must be absolute and unlimited also, at least so far forth as to make passive obedience and non-resistance a duty in all cases whatever, if not active obedience likewise. Though, by the way, there is here no distinction made between active and passive obedience; and if either of them be required in an unlimited sense, the other must be required in the same sense also, by virtue of the present argument, because the expressions are equally absolute with respect to both.

☙ Unlimited Obedience Questioned

But that unlimited obedience of any sort, cannot be argued merely from the indefinite expressions in which obedience is enjoined, appears from hence, that expressions of the same nature, frequently occur in Scripture, upon which it is confessed on all hands, that no such absolute and unlimited sense ought to be inferred. For example, *Love not the world; neither the things that are in the world* (1 John 2:15), *Lay not up for yourselves treasures upon earth* (Matthew. 6:19), and *Take therefore no thought for the morrow* (Matthew 6:34), are precepts expressed in at least equally absolute and unlimited terms. But it is generally allowed that they are to be understood with certain restrictions and limitations; some degree of love to the world and the things of it, being allowable. Nor, indeed, do the Right Reverend Fathers in God, and other dignified clergymen of the established [Anglican] church, seem to be altogether averse to admitting of restrictions in the latter case, how warm soever any of them may be against restrictions and limitations, in the case of submission to authority, whether civil of ecclesiastical. It is worth remarking also, that patience and submission under private injuries, are enjoined in much more peremptory and absolute terms than any that are used with regard to submission to the injustice and oppression of civil rulers. Thus, *I say unto you, that ye resist not evil; but whosoever shall smite thee on the right cheek, turn to him the other also. And if any man will sue thee at the law, and take away thy coat, let him have thy cloak also. And whosoever shall compel thee to go a mile with him, go with him twain* (Matthew 5:39-41). Any man may be defied to produce such strong expressions in favor of a passive and tame submission to unjust, tyrannical rulers, as are here used to enforce submission to private injuries. But how few are there that understand those expressions literally? And the reason why they do not, is because (with submission to the Quakers) common sense shows that they were not intended to be so understood.

℘ Family Government Illustrative

But to instance in some Scripture-precepts, which are more directly to the point in hand—children are commanded to obey their parents, and servants, their masters, in as absolute and unlimited terms as subjects are here commanded to obey their civil rulers. Thus, this same apostle—*Children obey your parents in the Lord; for this is right. Honor thy father and mother, which is the first commandment with promise—servants, be obedient to them that are your masters according to the flesh, with fear and trembling, with singleness of your heart as unto Christ* (Ephesians 6:1, etc.). Thus, also wives are commanded to be obedient to their husbands—Wives, submit yourselves unto your own husbands, as unto the Lord. For the husband is head of the wife, even as CHRIST IS THE HEAD OF THE CHURCH—*Therefore, as the church is subject unto Christ, so let the wives be to their own husbands* IN EVERYTHING (Ephesians 5:22-24). In all these cases, submission is required in terms (at least) as absolute and universal, as are ever used with respect to rulers and subjects. But who supposes that the apostle ever intended to teach that children, servants, and wives, should, in all cases whatever, obey their parents, masters, and husbands respectively, never making any opposition to their will, even although they should require them to break the commandments of God, or should causelessly make an attempt upon their lives? No one puts such a sense upon these expressions, however absolute and unlimited. Why then should it be supposed that the apostle designed to teach universal obedience, whether active or passive, to the higher powers merely because his precepts are delivered in absolute and unlimited terms? And if this be a good argument in one case, why is it not in others also? If it be said that resistance and disobedience to *the higher powers,* is here said positively to be a sin, so also is the disobedience of children to parents, servants to masters, and wives to husbands, in other places of Scripture. But the question still remains whether in all these cases there be not some exceptions? In the three latter, it is allowed there are. And from hence it follows that barely the use of absolute expressions is no proof, that obedience to civil rulers is, in all cases, a duty, or resistance, in all cases, a sin. I should not have thought it worthwhile to take any notice at all of this argument, had it not been much insisted upon by some

But who supposes that the apostle ever intended to teach that children, servants, and wives, should, in all cases whatever, obey their parents, masters, and husbands respectively?

of the advocates for passive obedience and non-resistance. For it is, in itself, perfectly trifling; and rendered considerable only by the stress that has been laid upon it for want of better.

ꙮ Unlimited Submission Not Intended

There is, indeed, one passage in the New Testament where it may seem, at first view, that an unlimited submission to civil rulers is enjoined: *Submit yourselves to every ordinance of man for the Lord's sake* (1 Peter 2:13)—To *every ordinance of man*. However, this expression is no stronger than that before taken notice of with relation to the duty of wives: *So, let the wives be subject to their own husbands*—IN EVERYTHING. But the true solution of this difficulty—if it be one—is this: by every ordinance of man,[26] is not meant every command of the civil magistrate without exception; but every order of magistrates appointed by man—whether superior or inferior, for so the apostle explains himself in the very next words—Whether it be to the king as supreme, or to governors, as unto them that are sent, &c. But although the apostle had not subjoined any such explanation, the reason of the thing itself would have obliged us to limit the expression [*every ordinance of man*] to such human ordinances and commands as are not inconsistent with the ordinances and commands of God, the supreme lawgiver; or with any other higher, and antecedent, obligations.

It is to be observed, in the next place, that as the duty of universal obedience and non-resistance to the *higher powers* cannot be argued from the absolute unlimited expressions

---

26 Literally, *every human institution, or appointment*. By which manner of expression, the apostle plainly intimates, that rulers derive their authority *Immediately*, not from *God*, but from *men*.

which the apostle here uses; so, neither can it be argued from the scope and drift of his reasoning, considered with relation to the persons he was here opposing. As was observed above, there were some professed *Christians* in the apostolic age, who disclaimed all magistracy and civil authority in general, *despising government*, and *speaking evil of dignities;* some under a notion that Jews ought not to be under the jurisdiction of *gentile* rulers; and others, that they were set *free* from the temporal powers, by Christ. Now it is with persons of this licentious opinion and character that the apostle is concerned. And all that was directly to his point, was to show that they were bound to submit to magistracy *in general.* This is a circumstance very material to be taken notice of, to ascertain the sense of the apostle. For this being considered, it is sufficient to account for all that he says concerning the duty of subjection, and the sin of resistance to the higher powers, without having recourse to the doctrine of unlimited submission and passive obedience, in all cases whatever. Were it known that those in opposition to whom the apostle wrote, allowed of civil authority in general, and only asserted that there were *some cases* in which obedience and non-resistance, were not a duty; there would, then, indeed, be reason for interpreting this passage as containing the doctrine of unlimited obedience, and non-resistance, as it must, in this case, be supposed to have been levelled against such as denied that doctrine. But since it is certain that there were persons who vainly imagined that civil government in general, was not to be regarded by them, it is most reason-

It is to be observed, in the next place, that as the duty of universal obedience and non-resistance to the higher powers cannot be argued from the absolute unlimited expressions which the apostle here uses.

able to suppose that the apostle designed his discourse only against them. And agreeably to this supposition, we find that he argues the usefulness of civil magistracy in general; its agreeableness to the will and purpose of God, who is *over all*; and so, deduces from hence, the obligation of submission to it. But it will not follow that because civil government is, in general, a good institution and necessary to the peace and happiness of human society, therefore there are no suppose able cases in which resistance to it can be innocent. So that the duty of unlimited obedience, whether active or passive, can be argued, neither from the manner of expression here used, nor from the general scope and design of the passage.

℘ Magistrates God's Ministers for Good

And if we attend to the nature of the argument with which the apostle here enforces the duty of submission to the *higher powers*, we shall find it to be such an one as concludes not in favor of submission to all who bear the title of rulers, in common, but only to those who actually perform the duty of rulers, by exercising a reasonable and just authority for the good of human society. This is a point which it will be proper to enlarge upon because the question before us turns very much upon the truth or falsehood of this position.

It is obvious then, in general, that the civil rulers whom the apostle here speaks of, and obedience to whom he presses upon Christians as a duty, are *good rulers*,[27] such as are, in the exercise of their office and power, benefactors to society. Such they are described to be throughout this passage. Thus,

---

27 By *good rulers*, are not intended such as are good in a *moral* or *religious*, but only in a *political*, sense; those who perform their duty so far as their office extends; and so far as civil society, as such, is concerned in their actions.

it is said, that they are not *a terror to good works, but to the evil;* that they are *God's ministers for good; revengers to execute wrath upon him that doth evil*; and that *they attend continually upon this very thing*. St. Peter gives the same account of rulers: They are *for a praise to them that do well, and the punishment of evil doers*.

℘ Magistrates "Not a Terror to Good Works"

If rulers are a terror to good works, and not to the evil; if they are not ministers for good to society, but for evil and distress, by violence and oppression; if they execute wrath upon sober, peaceable persons, who do their duty as members of society...they are not the same, but different persons from those whom St. Paul characterizes and who must be obeyed according to his reasoning.

It is manifest that this character and description of rulers, agrees only to such as are rulers in fact, as well as in name—to such as govern well, and act agreeably to their office. And the apostle's argument for submission to rulers, is wholly built and grounded upon a presumption that they do in fact answer this character; and is of no force at all upon supposition of the contrary. If *rulers are a terror to good works, and not to the evil*; if they are not *ministers for good to society*, but for evil and distress, by violence and oppression; if they *execute wrath upon* sober, peaceable persons, who do their duty as members of society; and suffer rich and honorable knaves to escape with impunity; if, instead of attending continually upon the good work of advancing the public welfare, they attend only upon the gratification of their own lust and pride and ambition, to the destruction of the public welfare. If this be the case, it is plain that the apostle's argument for submission does not reach them; they are not the same, but different persons from those whom he characterizes and who must be obeyed according to his reasoning.

Illustrated by Unfaithful Clergy

Let me illustrate the apostle's argument by the following similitude (it is no matter how far it is from anything which has, in fact, happened in the world). Suppose then, it was allowed, in general, that the *clergy* were a useful order of men; that they ought to be *esteemed very highly in love for their works sake* (1 Thessalonians 5:13) and to be decently supported by those whom they serve, *the laborer being worthy of his reward* (1 Timothy 5:18). Suppose farther that a number of Reverend and Right Reverend Drones, who worked not; who preached, perhaps, but once a year, and then, not the gospel of Jesus Christ, but the divine right of tithes— the dignity of their office as ambassadors of Christ, the equity of sinecures,[28] and a plurality of benefices—the excellency of the devotions in that prayer-book, which some of them hired chaplains to use for them—or some favorite point of church-tyranny and anti-Christian usurpation. Suppose such men as these, spending their lives in effeminacy, luxury and idleness; (or when they were not idle, doing that which is worse than idleness) suppose such men should merely, by the merit of ordination and consecration, and a peculiar, odd habit, claim great respect and reverence from those whom they civilly called the *beasts of the laity*[29] and demand thousands per annum for that good service which they—never performed; and for which, if they had per-

---

28 Employment, position, or office that requires little or no work but provides a salary.

29 Mr. Leslie

formed it, this would be much more than a quantum meruit. Suppose this should be the case, (it is only by way of simile, and surely it will give no offence) would not everybody be astonished at such insolence, injustice, and impiety? And ought not such men to be told plainly that they could not reasonably expect the esteem and reward due to the ministers of the gospel, unless they did the duties of their office? Should they not be told that their title and habit claimed no regard, reverence, or pay, separate from the care and work and various duties of their function? And that while they neglected the latter, the former served only to render them the more ridiculous and contemptible? The application of this similitude to the case in hand, is very easy.

℘ No Magisterial Authority to Do Mischief

If those who bear the title of civil rulers do not perform the duty of civil rulers but act directly counter to the sole end and design of their office; if they injure and oppress their subjects, instead of defending their rights and doing them good; they have not the least pretense to be honored, obeyed, and rewarded, according to the apostle's argument. For his reasoning, in order to show the duty of subjection to the higher powers is, as was before observed, built wholly upon the supposition that they do, in fact, perform the duty of rulers.

If it be said, that the apostle here uses another argument for submission to the higher powers, besides that which is taken from the usefulness of their office to civil society, when properly discharged and executed, namely, that their power is from God, that they are ordained of God and that they are God's ministers; and if it be said, that this argument for submission to them will hold good, although they do not exercise their power for the benefit, but for the ruin, and destruction of human society, this objection was obviated, in part, before. Rulers have no authority from God to do mischief. They are not God's ordinance, or God's ministers, in any other sense than as it is by his permission and providence that they are exalted to bear rule, and as magistracy duly exercised, and authority rightly applied, in the enacting and executing good laws, laws attempered and accommodated to the common welfare of the subjects, must be supposed to be agreeable to the will of the beneficent author and supreme Lord of the universe, whose kingdom ruleth over all (Psalm 103:19), and whose tender mercies are over all his works (Psalm 145:19). It is blasphemy to call tyrants and oppressors, God's ministers. They are more properly the messengers of Satan to buffet us (2 Corinthians 12:7). No rulers are properly God's ministers but such as are just, ruling in the fear of God (2 Samuel 23:3). When once magistrates act contrary to their office and the end of their institution, when they rob and ruin the public instead of being guardians of its peace and welfare, they immediately cease to be the ordinance and ministers of God and no more deserve that glorious character than common pirates and highwaymen. So that whenever that argument for submission fails, which is grounded upon the usefulness of magistracy to civil society, (as it always does when magistrates do hurt to society instead of good) the other argument, which is taken from their being the ordinance of God, must necessarily fail also, no person of a civil character being God's minister, in

When once magistrates act contrary to their office, and the end of their institution, when they rob and ruin the public, instead of being guardians of its peace and welfare, they immediately cease to be the ordinance and ministers of God and no more deserve that glorious character than common pirates and highwaymen.

the sense of the apostle, any farther than he performs God's will by exercising a just and reasonable authority and ruling for the good of the subject.

Let us now trace the apostle's reasoning in favor of submission to the higher powers a little more particularly and exactly. For by this, it will appear on one hand, how good and conclusive it is for submission to those rulers who exercise their power in a proper manner; and, on the other, how weak and trifling and unconnected it is—if it be supposed to be meant by the apostle to show the obligation and duty of obedience to tyrannical, oppressive rulers in common with others of a different character.

☙ Obedience to the Disobedient?

The apostle enters upon his subject thus: *Let every soul be subject unto the higher powers; for there is no power but of God: the powers that be, are ordained of God* (Verse 1). Here he urges the duty of obedience from this topic of argument, that civil rulers, as they are supposed to fulfil the pleasure of God, are the ordinance of God. But how is this an argument for obedience to such rulers as do not perform the pleasure of God by doing good, but the pleasure of the devil by doing evil; and such as are not, therefore, God's ministers, but the devil's! *Whosoever, therefore, resisteth the power, resisteth the ordinance of God; and they that resist, shall receive to themselves damnation* (Verse 2). Here the apostle argues that those who resist a reasonable and just authority, which is agreeable to the will of God, do really resist the will of God himself, and will, therefore, be punished by Him. But how does this prove that those who resist a lawless, unreasonable power, which is contrary to the will of God, do therein resist the will and ordinance of God? Is resisting those who resist God's will, the same thing with resisting God? Or shall those who do so, *receive to themselves damnation! For rulers are not a terror to good works, but to the evil. Wilt thou then not be afraid of the power? Do that which is good; and thou shalt have praise of the same. For he is the minister of God to thee for good* (Verse 3 and part of 4).

ꕥ Answering to the Divine Design of Government

Here the apostle argues more explicitly than he had before done for revering, and submitting to, magistracy from this consideration, that such as really performed the duty of magistrates, would be enemies only to the evil actions of men, and would befriend and encourage the good and so be a common blessing to society. But how is this an argument that we must honor and submit to such magistrates as are not enemies to the evil actions of men, but to the good; and such as are not a common blessing, but a common curse, to society! *But if thou do that which is evil, be afraid: For he is the minister of God, a revenger, to execute wrath upon him that doth evil* (Verse 4, latter part). Here the apostle argues from the nature and end of magistracy, that such as did evil, (and such only) had reason to be afraid of the higher powers, it being part of their office to punish evil doers, no less than to defend and encourage such as do well. But if magistrates are unrighteous; if they are respecters of persons; if they are partial in their administration of justice, then those who do well have as much reason to be afraid, as those that do evil. There can be no safety for the good, nor any peculiar ground of terror to the unruly and injurious. So that, in this case, the main end of civil government will be frustrated. And what reason is there for submitting to that government, which does by no means answer the design of government? *Wherefore ye must needs be subject not only for wrath, but also for conscience sake* (Verse 5).

Here the apostle argues the duty of a cheerful and conscientious submission to civil government from the nature and end of magistracy, as he had before laid it down, i.e., as the design of it was to punish evil doers and to support and encourage such as do well; and as it must, if so exercised, be agreeable to the will of God. But how does what he here says, prove the duty of a cheerful and conscientious subjection to those who forfeit the character of rulers—to those who encourage the bad, and discourage the good? The argument here used, no more proves it to be a sin to resist such rulers, than it does to *resist the devil,* that he may *flee from us* (James 4:7). For one is as truly the *minister of God* as the other. *For, this cause pay you tribute also; for they are God's ministers, attending continually upon this very thing* (Verse 6). Here the apostle argues the duty of paying taxes from this consideration, that those who perform the duty of rulers, are continually attending upon the public welfare. But how does this argument conclude for paying taxes to such princes as are continually endeavoring to ruin the public? And especially when such payment would facilitate and promote this wicked design! *Render therefore to all their dues; tribute, to whom tribute is due; custom, to whom custom; fear, to whom fear, honor, to whom honor* (Verse 7). Here the apostle sums up what he had been saying concerning the duty of subjects to rulers. And his argument stands thus—"Since magistrates who execute their office well, are common benefactors to society; and may, in that respect, be properly styled the ministers and ordinance of God; and since they are constantly employed in the service of the public; it becomes you to pay them tribute and custom; and to reverence, honor, and submit to them in the execution of their respective offices."

And what reason is there for submitting to that government, which does by no means answer the design of government?

☙ Should Taxes be Paid to Tyrants?

This is apparently good reasoning. But does this argument conclude for the duty of paying tribute, custom, reverence, honor, and obedience to such persons as (although they bear the title of rulers) use all their power to hurt and injure the public? Such as are not God's ministers, but Satan's? Such as do not take care of, and attend upon, the public interest, but their own, to the ruin of the public? That is, in short, to such as have no natural and just claim at all to tribute, custom, reverence, honor and obedience? It is to be hoped that those who have any regard to the apostle's character as an inspired writer, or even as a man of common understanding, will not represent him as reasoning in such a loose incoherent manner and drawing conclusions which have not the least relation to his premises. For what can be more absurd than an argument thus framed? "Rulers are, by their office, bound to consult the public welfare and the good of society: therefore, you are bound to pay them tribute, to honor, and to submit to them, even when they destroy the public welfare, and are common pest to society by acting in direct contradiction to the nature and end of their office."

☙ Governing for the Good of Society

Thus, upon a careful review of the apostle's reasoning in this passage, it appears that his arguments to enforce submission are of such a nature as to conclude only in favor of submission *to such rulers as he himself describes* (i.e., such as rule for the good of society, which is the only end of their institution). Common tyrants and public oppressors are not entitled to obedience from their subjects, by virtue of anything here laid down by the inspired apostle.

I now add, farther, that the apostle's argument is so far from proving it to be the duty of people to obey, and submit to, such rulers as act in contradiction to the public good,[30] and so to the design of their office, that it proves the direct contrary. For, please to observe, that if the end of all civil government be the good of society; if this be the thing that is aimed at in constituting civil rulers; and if the motive and argument for submission to government be taken from the apparent usefulness of civil authority; it follows that when no such good end can be answered by submission, there remains no argument or motive to enforce it; and if instead of this good end's being brought about by submission, a contrary end is brought about, and the ruin and misery of society effected by it, here is a plain and positive reason against submission in all such cases, should they ever happen. And therefore, in such cases, a regard to the public welfare, ought to make us withhold from our rulers that obedience and subjection which it would, otherwise, be our duty to render to them. If it be our duty, for example, to obey our king, merely for this reason, that he rules for the public welfare, (which is the only argument the apostle makes use of) it follows, by a parity of reason, that when he turns tyrant, and makes his subjects his prey to devour and to destroy, instead of his charge to defend and cherish, we are bound to throw off our allegiance to him and to resist; and that according to

> *Common tyrants, and public oppressors, are not entitled to obedience from their subjects, by virtue of anything here laid down by the inspired apostle.*

30 This does not intend, their acting so in a few particular instances, which the best of rulers may do through mistake, &c., but their acting so habitually and in a manner which plainly shows that they aim at making themselves great by the ruin of their subjects.

the tenor of the apostle's argument in this passage. Not to discontinue our allegiance in this case, would be to join with the sovereign in promoting the slavery and misery of that society, the welfare of which, we ourselves, as well as our sovereign, are indispensably obliged to secure and promote, as far as in us lies. It is true the apostle puts no case of such a tyrannical prince; but by his grounding his argument for submission wholly upon the good of civil society, it is plain he implicitly authorizes, and even requires us to make resistance, whenever this shall be necessary to the public safety and happiness. Let me make use of this easy and familiar similitude to illustrate the point in hand.

꧁ Illustration of Family Government

Suppose God requires a family of children to obey their father and not to resist him; and enforces his command with this argument; that the superintendence and care and authority of a just and kind parent, will contribute to the happiness of the whole family; so that they ought to obey him for their own sakes more than for his. Suppose this parent at length runs distracted and attempts, in his mad fit, to cut all his children's throats. Now, in this case, is not the reason before assigned, why these children should obey their parent while he continued of a sound mind, namely, *their common good,* a reason equally conclusive for disobeying and resisting him, since he is become delirious, and attempts their ruin? It makes no alteration in the argument, whether this parent properly speaking, loses his reason; or does, while he retains his understanding, that which is as fatal in its consequences, as anything he could do, were he really deprived of it. This similitude needs no formal application.

☙ Magistrates Subordinate to the Supreme Sovereign

But it ought to be remembered, that if the duty of universal obedience and non-resistance to our king or prince can be argued from this passage the same unlimited submission under a republican, or any other form of government, and even to all the subordinate powers in any particular state, can be proved by it as well, which is more than those who allege it for the mentioned purpose would be willing should be inferred from it. So that this passage does not answer their purpose, but really overthrows and confutes it. This matter deserves to be more particularly considered. The advocates for unlimited submission and passive obedience do, if I mistake not, always speak with reference to kingly or monarchical government as distinguished from all other forms; and, with reference to submitting to the will of the king in distinction from all subordinate officers acting beyond their commission and the authority which they have received from the crown. It is not pretended that any persons besides kings, have a divine right to do what they please, so that no one may resist them without incurring the guilt of factiousness and rebellion. If any other supreme powers oppress the people, it is generally allowed that the people may get redress by resistance, if other methods prove ineffectual. And if any officers in a kingly government go beyond the limits of that power

And if any officers in a kingly government, go beyond the limits of that power which they have derived from the crown (the supposed original source of all power and authority in the state) and attempt, illegally, to take away the properties and lives of their fellow-subjects, they may be forcibly resisted...

which they have derived from the crown (the supposed original source of all power and authority in the state) and attempt, illegally, to take away the properties and lives of their fellow-subjects, they may be forcibly resisted, at least till application can be made to the crown. But as to the sovereign himself, he may not be resisted in any case, nor any of his officers, while they confine themselves within the bounds which he has prescribed to them. This is, I think, a true sketch of the principles of those who defend the doctrine of passive obedience and non-resistance. Now there is nothing in Scripture which supports this scheme of political principles. As to the passage under consideration, the apostle here speaks of civil rulers in general; of all persons in common, vested with authority for the good of society without any particular reference to one form of government more than to another, or to the supreme power in any particular state, more than to subordinate powers. The apostle does not concern himself with the different forms of government.[31] This he supposes left entirely to hu-

31 The essence of government (I mean *good* government; and this is the *only* government which the apostle treats of in this passage) consists in the *making* and *executing of good laws*—laws attempered to the common felicity of the *governed.* And if this be, in *fact,* done, it is evidently, in itself, a thing of no consequence at all, what the particular form of government is— whether the legislative and executive power be lodged in *one and the same person,* or in *different* persons—whether in one person whom we call an *absolute monarch*—whether in a *few,* so as to constitute an aristocracy—whether in many, so as to constitute a *republic;* or whether in *three coordinate branches,* in such manner as to make the government *partake* something of each of these forms; and to be, at the same time, *essentially different* from them *all.* If the *end* be attained, it is enough. But no form of government seems to be so unlikely to accomplish this *end* as *absolute monarchy.* Nor is there

man prudence and discretion.

Now the consequence of this is that unlimited and passive obedience is no more enjoined in this passage under monarchical government, or to the supreme power in any state, than under all other species of government which answer the end of government; or, to all the subordinate degrees of civil authority, from the highest to the lowest. Those, therefore, who would from this passage infer the guilt of resisting kings in all cases whatever, though acting ever so contrary to the design of their office, must, if they will be consistent, go much farther and infer from it the guilt of resistance under all other forms of government and of resisting any petty officer in the state, though acting beyond his commission, in the most arbitrary, illegal manner possible. The argument holds equally strong in both cases. All civil rulers, as such, are the ordinance and ministers of God, and they are all, by the nature of their office, and in their respective spheres and stations, bound to consult the public welfare.

With the same reason, therefore, that any deny unlimited and passive obedience to be here enjoined under a republic or aristocracy, or any other established form of civil government; or to subordinate powers, acting in an illegal and oppressive manner, (with the same reason) others may deny that such obedience is enjoined to a king or monarch, or any civil power whatever. For the apostle says nothing that is peculiar to kings. What he says extends equally to all other persons

---

anyone that has so little pretense to a *divine original,* unless it be in this sense that God *first* introduced it into, and thereby overturned, the commonwealth of *Israel,* as a *curse* upon that people for their folly and wickedness, particularly in desiring such a government (see 1 Samuel 8). Just so God, before, sent *quails* amongst them as a *plague* and a *curse* and not as a *blessing* (Numbers 11).

whatever, vested with any civil office. They are all, in exactly the same sense, the ordinance of God; and the ministers of God; and obedience is equally enjoined to be paid to them all. For, as the apostle expresses it, there is No power but of God. And we are required to render to all their dues, and not more than their dues. And what these dues are, and to whom they are to be rendered, the apostle sayeth not; but leaves to the reason and consciences of men to determine.

Thus, it appears that the common argument grounded upon this passage in favor of universal and passive obedience, really overthrows itself by proving too much, if it proves anything at all. Namely, that no civil officer is, in any case whatever, to be resisted, though acting in express contradiction to the design of his office, which no man, in his senses, ever did, or can assert.

If we calmly consider the nature of the thing itself, nothing can well be imagined more directly contrary to common sense, than to suppose that millions of people should be subjected to the arbitrary, precarious pleasure of one single man, (who has naturally no superiority over them in point of authority) so that their estates, and everything that is valuable in life, and even their lives also, shall be absolutely at his disposal, if he happens to be wanton and capricious enough to demand them. What unprejudiced man can think that God made ALL to be thus subservient to

If we calmly consider the nature of the thing itself, nothing can well be imagined more directly contrary to common sense, than to suppose that millions of people should be subjected to the arbitrary, precarious pleasure of one single man so that their estates, and everything that is valuable in life shall be absolutely at his disposal.

the lawless pleasure and frenzy of ONE, so that it shall always be a sin to resist him! Nothing but the most plain and express revelation from heaven could make a sober, impartial man believe such a monstrous, unaccountable doctrine, and indeed, the thing itself appears so shocking, so out of all proportion, that it may be questioned whether all the miracles that ever were wrought, could make it credible, that this doctrine really came from God.

At present, there is not the least syllable in Scripture which gives any countenance to it. The hereditary, indefeasible, divine right of kings and the doctrine of non-resistance, which is built upon the supposition of such a right, are altogether as fabulous and fanciful as transubstantiation or any of the most absurd imaginative deceptions of ancient or modern visionaries. These notions are fetched neither from divine revelation, nor human reason, and if they are derived from neither of those sources, it does not much matter from whence they come or whither they go. Only it is a pity that such doctrines should be propagated in society to raise factions and rebellions, as we see they have been, in fact, both in the last and in the present REIGN.

But then, if unlimited submission and passive obedience to the *higher powers* in all possible cases is not a duty, it may be asked, "How far are we obliged to submit? If we may innocently disobey and resist in some cases, why not in all? Where shall we stop? What is the measure of our duty? This doctrine tends to the total dissolution of civil government and to introduce such scenes of wild anarchy and confusion, as are more fatal to society than the worst of tyranny."

After this manner, some men object and, indeed, this is the most plausible thing that can be said in favor of such an absolute submission as they plead for. But the worst (or rather the best) of it is, that there is very little strength or solidity in it. For similar difficulties maybe raised with respect to almost every duty of natural and revealed religion.

Two examples are relevant, both of which are near akin and indeed exactly parallel to the case before us. It is unquestionably the duty of children to submit to their parents, and of servants to their masters. But no one asserts that it is their duty to obey and submit to them in all supposable cases or universally a sin to resist them. Now does this tend to subvert the just authority of parents and masters or to introduce confusion and anarchy into private families? No. How then does the same principle tend to unhinge the government of that larger family, the body politic? We know, in general, that children and servants are obliged to obey their parents and masters respectively. We know also, with equal certainty, that they are not obliged to submit to them in all things, without exception, but may, in some cases, reasonably, and therefore innocently, resist them. These principles are acknowledged upon all hands, whatever difficulty there may be in fixing the exact limits of submission. Now there is at least as much difficulty in stating the measure of duty in these two cases, as in the case of rulers and subjects. So that this is really no objection—at least no reasonable one—against resistance to the higher powers or, if it is one, it will hold equally against resistance in the other cases mentioned. It is indeed true that turbulent, vicious-minded men may take occasion from this principle, that their rulers may, in some cases, be lawfully resisted, to raise factions and disturbances in the state, and to make resistance where resistance is needless, and therefore, sinful.

But is it not equally true, that children and servants of turbulent, vicious minds, may take occasion from this principle, that parents and masters may, in some cases be lawfully resisted, to resist when resistance is unnecessary, and therefore, criminal? Is the principle in either case false, merely because it may be abused and applied to legitimate disobedience and resistance in those instances to which it ought not to be applied? According to this way of arguing, there will be no true principles in the world, for there are none but what may be wrested and perverted to serve bad purposes, either through the weakness or wickedness of men.

The only reason of the institution of civil government; and the only rational ground of submission to it, is the common safety and

We may very safely assert these two things, in general, without undermining government. One is that no civil rulers are to be obeyed when they enjoin things that are inconsistent with the commands of God. All such disobedience is lawful and glorious; particularly, if persons refuse to comply with any legal establishment of religion because it is a gross perversion and corruption (as to doctrine, worship and discipline) of a pure and divine religion, brought from heaven to earth by the Son of God (the only King and Head of the Christian church) and propagated through the world by his inspired apostles. All commands running counter to the declared will of the supreme legislator of heaven and earth are null and void. And therefore, disobedience to them is a duty, not a crime.

Another thing that may be asserted with equal truth and safety is, that no government is to be submitted to at the expense of that which is the sole end of all government, the common good and safety of society. Because, to submit in this case, if it should ever happen, would evidently be to set up the means as more valuable and above the end, than which there cannot be a greater error and contradiction. The only reason of the institution of civil government; and the only rational ground of submission to it, is the common safety and utility. If therefore, in any case, the common safety and utility would not be promoted by submission to government, but the contrary, there is no ground or motive for obedience and submission but, for the contrary.

Whoever considers the nature of civil government is obliged to acknowledge that a great degree of implicit confidence must necessarily be placed in those that bear rule. This is implied in the very notion of authority being originally a trust, committed by the people to those who are vested with it—as all just and righteous authority is. Everything else is mere lawless force and usurpation. Neither God nor nature have given any man a right of dominion over any society, independent of that society's approbation and consent to be governed by him.

༻ Concerning Disobedience to Poor Management

Since all men are fallible, it cannot be supposed that the public affairs of any state are always administered in the best manner possible—even by persons of the greatest wisdom and integrity. Nor is disobedience to the higher powers legitimate when public affairs are not administered in the best possible manner or that they are, in some instances, very ill-managed, for upon this principle, it is scarcely supposable that any government at all could be supported or subsist. The belief that a poorly managed government legitimizes disobedience to that government manifestly tends to the disintegration of government and to throw all things into confusion and anarchy.

༻ Abuse of Power Forfeits Obedience

But it is equally evident, upon the other hand, that those in authority may abuse their trust and power to such a degree that neither the law of reason, nor of religion, requires that any obedience or submission should be paid to them. But, on the contrary, that they should be totally discarded and the authority which they possessed transferred to others, who may exercise it more to those good purposes for which it is given.

℘ Misuse of Principle of Disobedience Rare

Nor is the charge that this principle of justifiable resistance to higher powers (in some extraordinary cases) liable to abuse—as many persons seem to believe. For although there will always be some petulant, querulous men, in every state—men of factious, turbulent, and carping dispositions, glad to lay hold of any trifle to justify and legitimize their caballing against their rulers, and other seditious practices, yet there are, comparatively speaking, but few men of this contemptible character. It appears that mankind in general, has a disposition to be as submissive and passive and tame under government as they ought to be.

Consider the fact that a great—if not the greatest—part of the known world who are now groaning, but not murmuring, under the heavy yoke of tyranny! While those who govern, do it with any tolerable degree of moderation and justice and in any good measure act up to their office and character by being public benefactors, the people will generally be easy and peaceable and be rather inclined to flatter and adore, than to insult and resist them. Nor was there ever any general complaint against any administration which lasted long, but what there was good reason.

℘ People Able to Discern Good Government

Till people find themselves greatly abused and oppressed by their governors, they are not apt to complain, and whenever they do, in fact, find themselves thus abused and oppressed, they must be stupid not to complain. To say that subjects in general are not proper judges when their governors oppress them and play the tyrant, or when they defend their rights, administer justice impartially, and promote the public welfare is as great a treason as ever man uttered. 'Tis treason, not against one single man, but the state—against the whole body politic; 'tis treason against mankind; 'tis treason against common sense; 'tis treason against God. And this impious principle lays the foundation for justifying all the tyranny and oppression that ever any prince was guilty of.

The people know for what purpose they set up and maintain their governors; and they are the proper judges when they execute their trust as they ought to do...

The people know for what purpose they set up and maintain their governors; and they are the proper judges when they execute their trust as they ought to do it—when their prince exercises an equitable and paternal authority over them—when from a prince and common father, he exalts himself into a tyrant—when from subjects and children, he degrades them into the class of slaves—plunders them, makes them his prey, and unnaturally sports himself with their lives and fortunes!

A people oppressed to a great degree by their sovereign cannot be insensitive to the fact that they are oppressed. And such a people—if I may allude to an ancient fable—have, like the Hesperian fruit, a dragon for their protector and guardian; nor, would they have any reason to mourn if some Hercules should appear to dispatch him, for a nation thus abused to arise unanimously, and to resist their prince, even to the dethroning him, is not criminal, but a reasonable way of vindicating their liberties and just rights. It is making use of the means—and the only means—which God has put into their power for mutual and self-defense. And it would be highly criminal in them not to make use of this means. It would be stupid tameness, and unaccountable folly for whole nations to suffer one unreasonable, ambitious, and cruel man to wanton and riot in their misery. And in such a case, it would, of the two, be more rational to suppose that they who did not resist—than that they who did—would receive to themselves damnation.

SECTION TWO

The Extent to Which Government May Be Resisted

Historical Setting

King Charles I

And, this naturally brings us to make some reflections upon the resistance which was made about a century since to that unhappy prince, ***King Charles I,*** and upon the anniversary of his death. This is a point which I should not have concerned myself about were it not that some men continue to speak of it, even to this day, with a great deal of warmth and zeal and in such a manner as to undermine all the principles of liberty, whether civil or religious, and to introduce the most abject slavery, both in church and state, so that it has become a matter of universal concern. What I have to offer upon this subject will be comprised in a short answer to the following queries, namely:

For what reason the resistance to King Charles I was made? By whom it was made? Whether this resistance was rebellion[32] or not? How the anniversary of King Charles's death came at first to be solemnized as a day of fasting and humiliation? And lastly, why those of the episcopal clergy who are very high in the principles of ecclesiastical authority continue to speak of this unhappy man as a great saint and a martyr?

℘ Why Was King Charles Resisted?

For what reason then, was the resistance to King Charles made? The general answer to this inquiry is that it was on account of the tyranny and oppression of his reign. Not a great while after his accession to the throne, he married a French Catholic, ***Henrietta Maria***, and with her seemed to have wedded the politics, if not the religion of France, also. For afterwards, during a reign—or rather a tyranny of many years—he governed in a

Henrietta Maria

32 N. B. I speak of rebellion, treason, saintship, martyrdom, &c. throughout this discourse, only in the scriptural and theological sense. I know not how the law defines them; the study of that not being my employment.

perfectly wild and arbitrary manner, paying no regard to the constitution and the laws of the kingdom by which the power of the crown was limited or to the solemn oath which he had taken at his coronation. It would be endless, as well as needless, to give a particular account of all the illegal and despotic measures which he took in his administration—partly from his own natural lust of power and partly from the influence of wicked counselors and ministers. He committed many illustrious members of both houses of Parliament to the tower for opposing his arbitrary schemes. He levied many taxes upon the people without consent of Parliament and then imprisoned great numbers of the principal merchants and gentry for not paying them.

William Laud

He erected, or at least revived, several arbitrary courts in which the most unheard-of barbarities were committed with his knowledge and approbation. He supported that more than fiend, ***Archbishop William Laud,*** and the clergy of his stamp in all their church tyranny and hellish cruelties. He authorized a book in favor of sports upon the Lord's Day, and several clergymen were persecuted by him and the mentioned pious bishop for not reading it to the people after divine service. When the Parliament complained to him of the arbitrary proceedings of his corrupt ministers, he told that august body in a rough, domineering, unprincely manner that he wondered anyone should be so foolish and insolent as to think that he would part with the meanest of his servants upon their account. He refused to call any Parliament at all for the space of twelve years together, during all which time, he governed in an absolute lawless and despotic manner. He took all opportunities to encourage the papists, and to promote them to the highest offices of honor and trust. He (probably) abetted the horrid massacre in Ireland, in which two hundred thousand Protestants were butchered by the Roman Catholics. He sent a large sum of money which he had raised by his arbitrary taxes into Germany, to raise foreign troops to force more arbitrary taxes upon his subjects. He not only by a long series of actions, but also in plain terms, asserted an absolute uncontrollable power, saying even in one of his speeches to Parliament that as it was blasphemy to dispute what God might do; so, it was sedition in subjects to dispute what the king might do.

Towards the end of his tyranny, he came to the house of commons with an armed force[33] and demanded five of its principal members to be delivered up to him. And this was a prelude to that unnatural war which he soon after levied against his own dutiful subjects whom he was bound by all the laws of honor, humanity, piety, and I might add, of interest also, to defend and cherish with a paternal affection. I have only time to hint at these facts in a general way, all which and many more of the same tenor, may be proved by good authorities, so that the figurative language which St. John uses concerning the just and beneficent deeds of our blessed Savior, may be applied to the unrighteous and execrable deeds of this prince, personally: *And there are also many other things which King Charles did, the which, if they should be written everyone, I suppose that even the world itself, could not contain the*

33 Historians are not agreed what number of soldiers attended him in this monstrous invasion of the privileges of Parliament. Some say 500, some 400, and the author of *The History of the Kings of Scotland*, says 500.

books that should be written (John 21:25). Now it was on account of King Charles's efforts to assume power above the laws—in direct contradiction to his coronation oath—and with which he governed the greatest part of his reign in the most arbitrary oppressive manner, that resistance was made against him, which—in due time—resulted in the loss of his crown and of that head which was unworthy to wear it.

✠ Who Resisted King Charles?

But by whom was this resistance made? Not by a private junto; not by a small seditious party; not by a few desperadoes who, to mend their fortunes, would embroil the state, but by the Lords and Commons of England. It was they that almost unanimously opposed the king's measures for overturning the constitution and changing that free and happy government into a wretched absolute monarchy. It was they, that when the king was about levying forces against his subjects—to make himself absolute—commissioned officers and raised an army to defend themselves and the public. And it was they that maintained the war against him all along till he was made a prisoner. This is indisputable. Though it was not properly speaking the Parliament, but the army, which put him to death afterwards. And it ought to be freely acknowledged that most of their proceeding to get this matter effected—and particularly the court by which the king was at last tried and condemned—was little better than a mere mockery of justice.

✠ Was This Resistance a Rebellion?

The next question which naturally arises, is whether this resistance, which was made to the king by the Parliament, was properly a rebellion, or not? The answer to which is plain, that it was not but a most righteous and glorious stand, made in defense of the natural and legal rights of the people against the unnatural and illegal encroachments of arbitrary power. Nor was this a rash and too sudden opposition. The nation had been patient under the oppressions of the crown, even to longsuffering for a course of many years, and there was no rational hope of redress in any other way. Resistance was absolutely necessary in order to preserve the nation from slavery, misery, and ruin. And who so proper to make this resistance as the lords and commoners, the whole representative body of the people—guardians of the public welfare; and each of which was, in point of legislation, vested with an equal, coordinate power, with that of the crown?

Resistance was absolutely necessary in order to preserve the nation from slavery, misery, and ruin.

To momentarily digress, the English constitution is originally and essentially free. The character which Julius Cesar and Tacitus both give of the ancient Britain's so long ago is that they were extremely jealous of their liberties, as well as a people of a martial spirit. Nor have there been wanting frequent instances and proofs of the same glorious spirit (in both respects) remaining in their posterity ever since in the struggles they have made for liberty, both against foreign and domestic tyrants. Their kings hold their title to the throne solely by grant of Parliament (i.e., in other words, by the voluntary consent of the people). And, agreeably hereto, the prerogative and rights of the crown are stated, defined, and limited by law and that as truly and strictly as the rights of any inferior officer in the state, or indeed, of any private subject. And it is only in this respect that it can be said that "the king can do no wrong." Being restrained by the law, he cannot—while he confines himself within those just limits which the law prescribes to him as the measure of his authority—injure and oppress the subjects of his realm.

The king, in his coronation oath, swears to exercise only such a power as the constitution gives him. And the subject, in the oath of allegiance, swears only to obey him in the exercise of such a power. The king is as much bound by his oath not to infringe the legal rights of the people as the people are bound to yield subjection to him. From this it follows, that as soon as the prince sets himself up above law, he loses the king in the tyrant. He does to all intents and purposes unking himself by acting out of and beyond that sphere which the constitution allows him to move in. And in such cases, he has no more right to be obeyed than any inferior officer who acts beyond his commission. The subject's obligation to allegiance then ceases of course, and to resist him, is no more rebellion than to resist any foreign invader.

There is an essential difference between government and tyranny, at least under such a constitution as the English. The former consists in ruling according to law and equity, the latter in ruling contrary to law and equity. So also, there is an essential difference between resisting a tyrant, and rebellion. The former is a just and reasonable self-defense; the latter consists in resisting a prince whose administration is just and legal, and this is what denominates it a crime. Now it is evident, that King Charles's government was illegal and very oppressive through the greatest part of his reign. And therefore, to resist him was no more rebellion, than to oppose any foreign invader, or any other domestic oppressor.

Returning to our main point, Parliament is composed of two bodies of governors, the lords and commoners, the whole representative body of the people—guardians of the public welfare. Here were two branches of the legislature against the one (the king)—two, which had law and equity and the constitution on their side, against one which was impiously attempting to overturn law and equity and the constitution and to exercise a wanton licentious sovereignty over the properties, consciences, and lives of all the people.

Such a sovereignty, as some inconsiderately ascribe to the supreme governor of the world, I say, inconsiderately because God himself does not govern in an absolutely arbitrary and despotic manner. The power of this Almighty King (I speak it not without caution and reverence—the power of this Almighty King) is limited by law—not, indeed, by acts of Parliament, but by the eternal laws of truth, wisdom, equity, and the everlasting tables of right reason—tables that cannot be repealed or thrown down and broken like those of Moses. But King Charles sat himself up above all these, as much as he did above the written laws of the realm, and made mere pleasure and whim—which are no rule at all—the only rule and measure of his administration.

And now, is it not perfectly ridiculous to call resistance to such a tyrant by the name of rebellion—the grand rebellion? Even that—Parliament which brought ***King Charles II*** to the throne, and which run loyally mad, severely reproved one of their own members for condemning the proceedings of that Parliament which first took up arms against the former king. And upon the same principles that the proceedings of this Parliament may be censured as wicked and rebellious, the

Charles II

proceedings of those who since, opposed King James II and brought ***William III Prince of Orange*** to the throne, may be censured as wicked and rebellious also. The cases are parallel. But whatever some men may think, it is to be hoped that, for their own sakes, they will not dare to speak against the Revolution upon the justice and legality of which depends (in part) his present majesty's right to the throne.

William III of Orange

If it is said that, although the Parliament which first opposed King Charles's measures and eventually took up arms against him was not guilty of rebellion, yet certainly those persons were, who condemned and put him to death—though even this perhaps is not true. For he had, in fact, unkinged himself long before and had forfeited his title to the allegiance of the people. So that those who put him to death were at most only guilty of murder which, indeed, is bad enough if they were guilty of that—which is at least disputable. ***Oliver Cromwell***, and those who were principally concerned in the nominal king's death, might possibly have been very wicked and

Oliver Cromwell

designing men. Nor shall I say anything in vindication of the reigning hypocrisy of those times or of Cromwell's maladministration during the interregnum, for it is truth and not a party for which I am speaking. But still it may be said that Cromwell and his adherents were not, properly speaking, guilty of rebellion because he, whom they beheaded was not, properly speaking, their king, but a lawless tyrant. Much less is the whole body of the nation at that time to be charged with rebellion on that account, for it was no national act. It was not done by a free Parliament. And much less still is the nation at present to be charged with the great sin of rebellion for what their ancestors did—or rather did not—a century ago.

☙ Concerning the Canonization of Charles I

But how did the anniversary of King Charles's death come to be solemnized as a day of fasting and humiliation? The true answer, in brief, is that this fast was instituted by way of court and complement to King Charles II upon the Restoration. All were desirous of paying homage to him, of ingratiating themselves, and of making him forget what had been done in opposition to his father so as not to revenge it. To affect this, they ran into the most extravagant professions of affection and loyalty to him, insomuch that he himself said that it was a mad and hair brained loyalty which they professed. And amongst other strange things which his first Parliament did, they ordered the Thirtieth of January—the day on which his father was beheaded—to be kept as a day of solemn humiliation, to announce the judgments of heaven for the rebellion which the nation had been guilty of, which was no national decision, and which was not rebellion in them that did it. Thus, they soothed and flattered their new king at the expense of their liberties and were ready to surrender freely to Charles II all that enormous power with which they had justly resisted Charles I for usurping to himself.

Concerning Kowtowing of Anglican Clergy

The last query mentioned, was why those of the Anglican clergy, who are very high in the principles of ecclesiastical authority, continue to speak of this unhappy prince as a great saint and a martyr? This, we know, is what they constantly do, especially upon the 30th of January—a day sacred for the purpose of extolling him and for reproaching those who are not of the established church. Out of the same mouth on this day, proceedeth blessing and cursing (James 3:8-10), therewith bless they their God—even Charles—and therewith curse they, the dissenters, who were responsible for the execution of King Charles. And their tongue can no man tame; it is an unruly evil, full of deadly poison. King Charles is upon this solemn occasion frequently compared to our Lord Jesus Christ, both in respect of the holiness of his life and the greatness and injustice of his sufferings, and it is a wonder they do not add something concerning the merits of his death also. But blessed saint and royal martyr are as humble titles as any that are thought worthy of him.

> *Is there any such thing as grace without goodness—as being a follower of Christ without following Him; as being his disciple, without learning of him—to be just and beneficent, or as saintship without sanctity?*

Now this may at first view well appear to be a very strange phenomenon. For King Charles was really a man black with guilt and laden with iniquity (Isaiah 1:4), as appears by his crimes before mentioned. He lived a tyrant, and it was the oppression and violence of his reign that brought him to his untimely and violent end at last. Now what of saintship or martyrdom is there in all this? What of saintship is there in encouraging people to profane the Lord's Day? What of saintship in falsehood and perjury? What of saintship in repeated robberies and depredations? What of saintship in throwing real saints and glorious patriots into prison? What of saintship in overturning an excellent civil constitution and proudly grasping at an illegal and monstrous power? What of saintship in the murder of thousands of innocent people and involving a nation in all the calamities of a civil war? And what of martyrdom is there in a man's bringing an immature and violent death upon himself by being wicked overmuch (Ecclesiastes 7:17)? Is there any such thing as grace without goodness—as being a follower of Christ without following Him; as being His disciple, without learning of Him to be just and beneficent—or as saintship without sanctity?[34] If not, I fear it will be hard to prove this man a saint. And certainly, one would be apt to suspect that the Anglican Church must be but poorly stocked

[34] Is it any wonder that even persons who do not walk after their own lusts, should scoff at such saints as this, both in the first and in the last days, even from everlasting to everlasting? (2 Peter 3:3, 4) But perhaps it will be said that these things are MYSTERIES, which (although very true in themselves) lay-understandings cannot comprehend or, indeed, any other persons amongst us, besides those who being INWARDLY MOVED BY THE HOLY GHOST, have taken a trip across the Atlantic to obtain episcopal ordination and the indelible character. However, if these consecrated gentlemen do not quite despair of us, it is hoped that in the abundance of their charity, they will endeavor to elucidate these dark points; and, at the same time, explain the creed of another of their eminent saints, which we are told, that unless we believe faithfully, (i.e. believingly) we cannot be saved, which creed, (or rather riddle) notwithstanding all the labors of the pious—and metaphysical Dr. Waterland, remains somewhat enigmatical still.

with saints and martyrs which is forced to adopt such enormous sinners into her calendar to swell the number.

But when attempting to unravel this mystery of nonsense as well as of iniquity which has already worked for a long time amongst us (2 Thessalonians 2:7), or at least to give the most probable solution to it, it is to be remembered, that King Charles, this burlesque upon saintship and martyrdom, though so great an oppressor, was a true friend to the Anglican Church—so true a friend to her that he was very well affected towards the Roman Catholics and would probably have been very willing to unite Lambeth and Rome. This appears by his marrying a true daughter of that true mother of harlots (Revelation 17:5), which he did with a dispensation from the Pope, that supreme bishop to whom when he wrote, he gave the title of "most holy Father." His queen was extremely bigoted to all the follies and superstitions and to the hierarchy of Rome and had a prodigious ascendency over him all his life. It was, in part, owing to this that he probably abetted the massacre of the Protestants in Ireland; that he assisted in extirpating the French Protestants at Rochelle; that he all along encouraged papists, and popishly effected clergymen, in preference to all other persons; and that he upheld that monster of wickedness, Archbishop Laud, and the bishops of his stamp in all their church-tyranny and diabolical cruelties.

In return for his kindness and indulgence in which respects, they caused many of the pulpits throughout the nation to ring with the divine absolute, indefeasible right of kings, with the praises of Charles and his reign, and with the damnable sin of resisting the Lord's anointed, let him do what he would. So that not Christ, but Charles, was commonly preached to the people. In plain English, there seems to have been an impious bargain struck up between the scepter and the surplice for enslaving both the bodies and souls of men. The king appeared to be willing that the clergy should do what they would: set up a monstrous hierarchy like that of Rome, a monstrous inquisition like that of Spain or Portugal, or anything else which their own pride, and the devil's malice, could prompt them to—provided always that the clergy would be tools to the crown; that they would make the people believe that kings had God's authority for breaking God's law; that they had a commission from heaven to seize the estates and lives of their subjects at pleasure; and that it was a damnable sin to resist them, even when they did such things as deserved more than damnation.

This appears to be the true key for explaining the mysterious doctrine of King Charles's saintship and martyrdom. He was a saint, not because he was in his life a good man, but a good churchman; not because he was a lover of holiness, but the hierarchy; not because he was a friend to Christ, but the priest-craft. And he was a martyr in his death, not because he bravely suffered death in the cause of truth and righteousness, but because he died an enemy to liberty and the rights of conscience; not because he died an enemy to sin, but dissenters—Christians outside of the Anglican Church in English lands. For these reasons it is that all bigoted clergymen and friends to church-power paint this man as a saint in his life, though he was such a mighty, such a royal sinner, and as a martyr in his death, though he fell a sacrifice only to his own ambition, avarice, and unbounded lust of power.

And from prostituting their praise upon King Charles and offering him that incense, which is not his due, it is natural for them to make a transition to the dissenters, as they commonly do, and to heap reproach upon them which they do not deserve—they are generally professed enemies both to civil and ecclesiastical tyranny. We are commonly charged (on the thirtieth of January) with the guilt of putting the king to death under a notion that it was our ancestors that did it, and so, we are represented in the blackest colors, not only as schismatics, but also as traitors and rebels and all that is bad. And these lofty gentlemen usually rail upon this head in such a manner as plainly shows, that they are either grossly ignorant of the history of those times which they speak of, or which is worse, that they are guilty of the most shameful prevarication, slander, and falsehood. But every petty priest with a roll and a gown thinks he must do something in imitation of his betters—in attire—and show himself a true son of the church. And thus, through a foolish ambition to appear considerable, they only render themselves contemptible.

This appears to be the true key for explaining the mysterious doctrine of King Charles's saintship and martyrdom. He was a saint, not because he was in his life a good man, but a good churchman; not because he was a lover of holiness, but the hierarchy; not because he was a friend to Christ, but the priest-craft.

But suppose our forefathers did kill their mock saint and martyr a century ago, what is that to us now? If I mistake not, these gentlemen generally preach down the doctrine of the imputation of Adam's sin to his posterity as absurd and unreasonable, notwithstanding they have solemnly subscribed what is equivalent to it in their own articles of religion. And therefore, one would hardly expect that they would lay the guilt of the king's death upon us, although our forefathers had been the only authors of it. But this conduct is much more surprising when it does not appear that our ancestors had any more hand in it than their own. However, bigotry is sufficient to account for this and many other phenomena which cannot be accounted for in any other way.

Although the observation of this anniversary seems to have been at least superstitious in its original, and although it is often abused to very bad purposes by the established clergy—as they serve their own self-interest to perpetuate strife, a party spirit, and divisions in the Christian church—yet it is to be hoped that one good end will be answered by it, quite contrary to their intention. It is to be hoped, that it will prove a standing memento that Britons will not be slaves, and a warning to all corrupt counselors and ministers not to go too far in advising to arbitrary, despotic measures.

☙ Conclusion: Loyalty and Liberty

To conclude, let us all learn to be free and to be loyal. Let us not profess ourselves vassals to the lawless pleasure of any man on earth. But let us remember, at the same time, government is sacred and not to be trifled with. It is our happiness to live under the government of a prince who is satisfied with ruling according to law as every other good prince will. We enjoy under his administration all the liberty that is proper and expedient for us. It becomes us, therefore, to be contented and dutiful subjects. Let us prize our freedom but not use our liberty for a cloak of maliciousness (1 Peter 2:16). There are men who strike at liberty under the term licentiousness. There are others who aim at popularity under the disguise of patriotism. Be aware of both. Extremes are dangerous. There is at present amongst us, perhaps, more danger of the latter, than of the former. For which reason I would exhort you to pay all due regard to the government over us, to the king and all in authority, and to lead a quiet and peaceable life (1 Timothy 2:2).

And while I am speaking of loyalty to our earthly Prince, suffer me just to put you in mind to be loyal also to the supreme RULER of the universe, by whom kings reign and princes decree justice (Proverbs 8:15). To which king eternal, immortal, invisible, even to the only wise God (2 Timothy 1:2), be all honor and praise, dominion, and thanksgiving, through JESUS CHRIST our LORD. AMEN.

F I N I S

www.ingramcontent.com/pod-product-compliance
Ingram Content Group UK Ltd.
Pitfield, Milton Keynes, MK11 3LW, UK
UKHW022013190726
13853UKWH00005B/1911

9 798434 852128